Rumors to Wake Up To
Barry Schwabsky

artwork
t thilleman

SPUYTEN DUYVIL
NEW YORK CITY

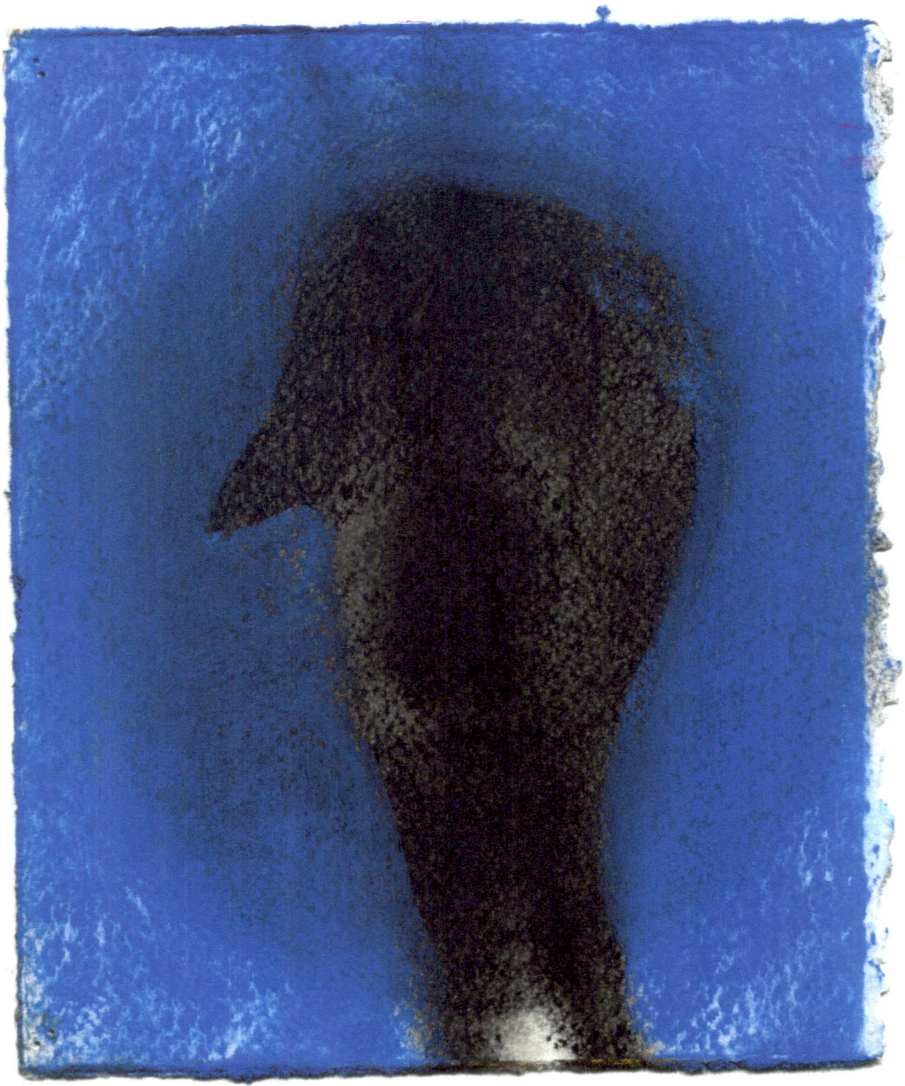

Dust-colored sea bird afloat

against a contrary wind

solitary eye at rest in its hollow

None to whom lament be addressed

the sky being beauty wherever

my other body: the imponderable

Noon—resplendent!—and answering lights

inside your skin, so stark

this apparition won't appear anymore

Ladder I'll never climb down

destination: mirrored moon or mortal man

the only fall would be mine into a trance

Infinite enclosure just feet above the world

wonder how we got here

long days of caresses energy flows through

We bury time in aromas

forgetting I don't know what sort of thing I could be,

what sort I no longer am, a flickering presence

A shadow stretched so eagerly

what bed ever saw a thing like that

your pet voice turns to lick its wounds

Began thinking as a bird and never finished

said once it's as tears that time flows

through cracks between broken porcelain syllables

From what measured distance dare watch you live

demon songs leaking out all over

lave my evil eye, rod and cone alike

Wondering where longing bears its fruit

a childhood spent in secret

still waits for the incandescent message of the solstice

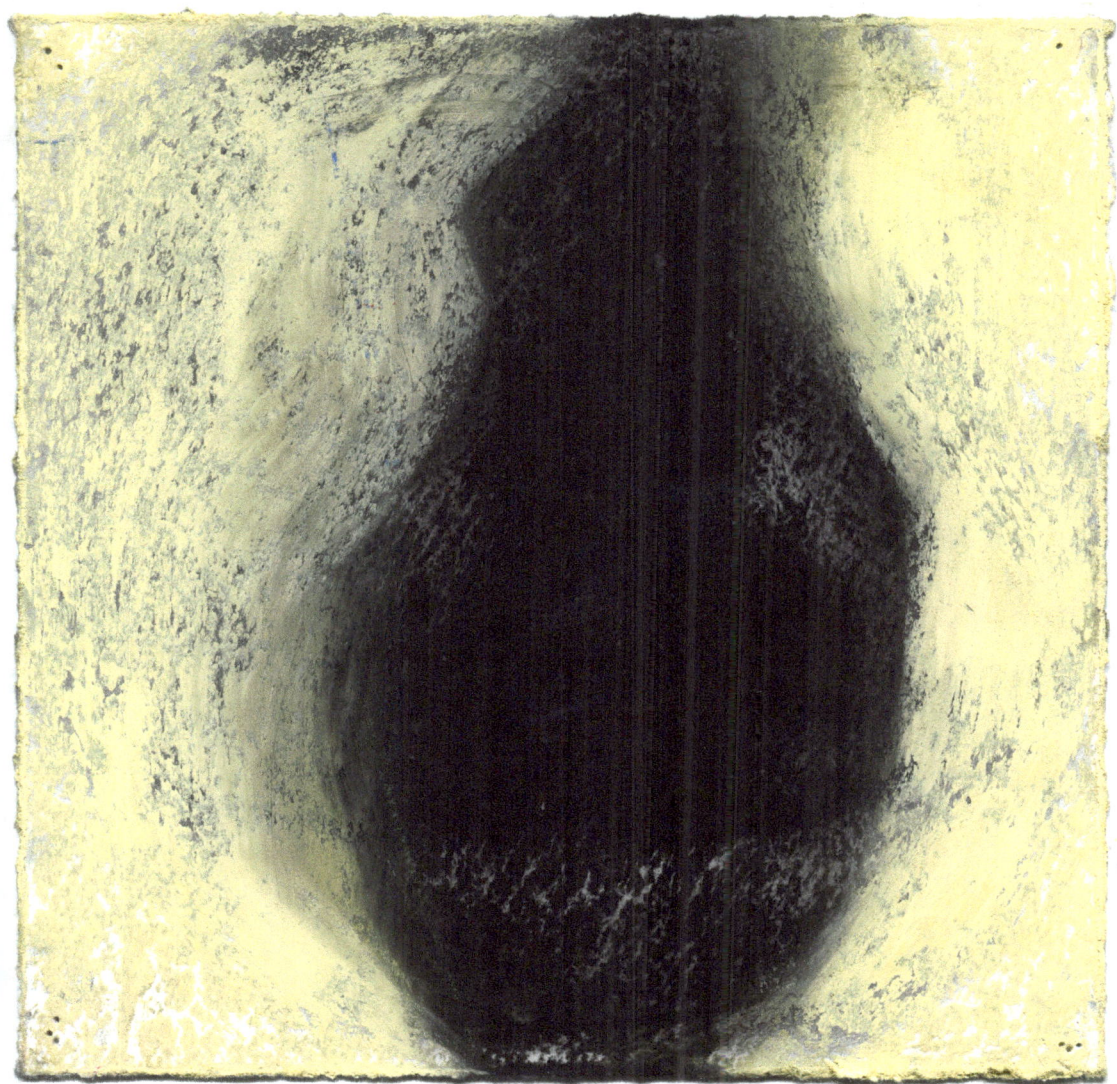

Is it really all about the feedback

our animus against the merely true

this question for whoever can answer it

The sun stops here and now

under skies of intense loneliness

no destiny in hand, a poet might never have existed

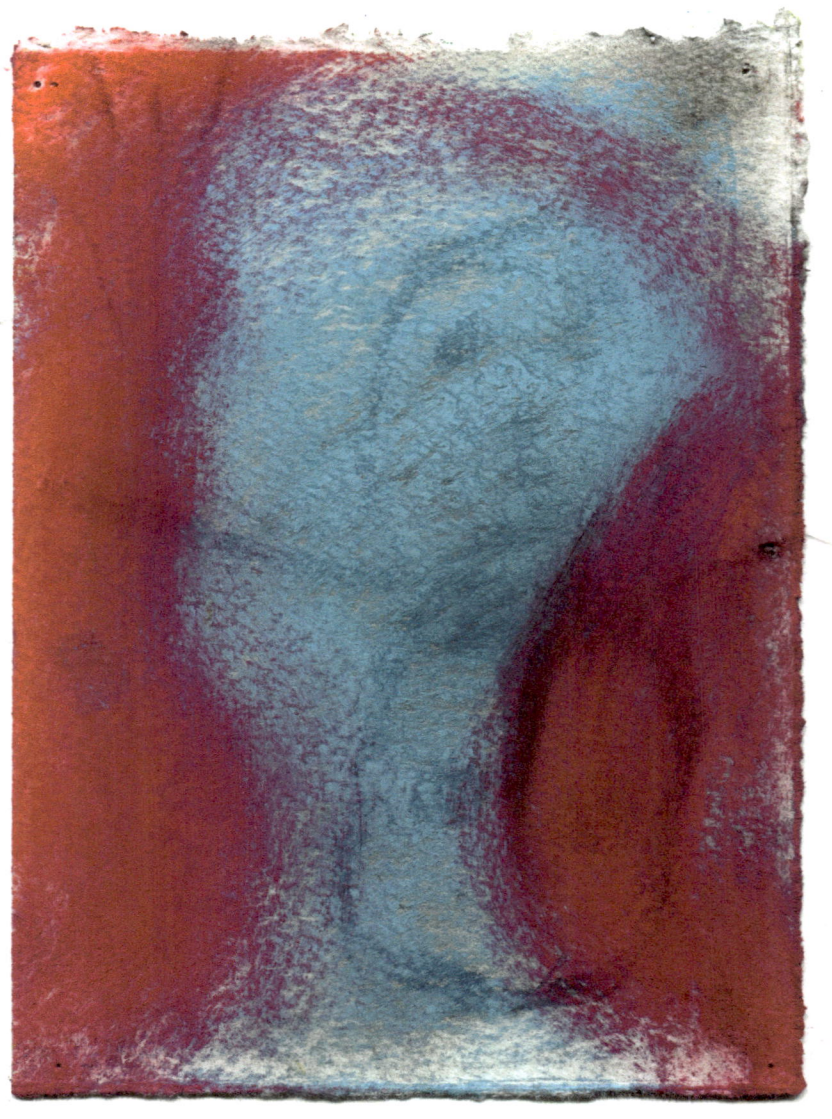

Wondering the same about other people

blue, insatiable, discerns a tree without a face

you lose the art of getting closer to the end

www.ingramcontent.com/pod-product-compliance
Lightning Source LLC
Chambersburg PA
CBHW041605120626
46551CB00002B/321